Keys to the Past

Series Editor: Edith Freeman, B.A.

Victorian Life and transport

Richard Dunning, B.A.
Humanities Co-ordinator,
All Saints Middle School,
Sudbury, Suffolk.

Acknowledgements

The author wishes to thank Steve Bixley, Paul Frankland, Nic Kent and also the staff of the Suffolk Record Office, Bury St Edmunds, for their assistance. The Publishers acknowledge with thanks the co-operation of the Museum of London and the assistance of John Edwards, Chris Ellmers and Barry Grey.

The photographs on pages 3 (top left) and 44 (bottom) are reproduced by gracious permission of Her Majesty the Queen: copyright reserved.

Acknowledgements for other photographs are due to the following:

Ian Allan Ltd: 13 (bottom), 41 (bottom right); J. Allan Cash Ltd: 16 (top right), 40 (centre), 44 (top); Barnaby's Picture Library: 6 (top left); BBC Hulton Picture Library: 8 (centre), 15 (left), 27; Beecroft Art Gallery, Southend-on-Sea: 44 (centre); R. Benton/Tramway Museum, Crich: 20 (centre); Blue Circle Industries/Hutchinson – from *Your House – The Outside View* by John Prizeman: 32 (top and centre); British Rail, Western Region: 12 (top right); British Waterways Board: 6 (top right), 7 (top left and right) ; Canadian Pacific: 39 (bottom right); Castle Museum, York; 33 (top right); Collection of Edwin Course: 36 (bottom); J. H. Cooper-Smith: 13 (top); Fotomas Index: 8 (bottom), 10 (centre), 12 (centre), 30 (bottom), inside back cover (top); Peter Green: 3 (right), 7 (centre), 34 (left); Guildhall Library, City of London: 8 (top right), 48; Brian Haresnape: 16 (bottom); *Illustrated London News* Picture Library: 18 (bottom), 22 (left), 23 (top); John Topham Picture Library: 14 (top); A. P. Judd: 20 (top); London Transport Executive: 19 (bottom), 21 (top and bottom); London Transport Museum: title page; Mansell Collection: 5 (bottom), 9 (bottom), 10 (bottom left and right), 11 (bottom left and right), 31 (top), 34 (right), 35 (top), 39 (centre), 43 (top), 47 (top and bottom), inside back cover (centre left, centre right, bottom left and bottom right); Mary Evans Picture Library: 19 (top), 31 (bottom), 32 (bottom): National Motor Museum, Beaulieu: 22 (right); National Railway Museum, York – Crown Copyright: inside front cover, 11 (top), 12 (bottom left), 24 (bottom), 28 (bottom left and right), 41 (left, centre left and right), 42 (left); P & O: 46 (bottom); Press Association: 40 (top); River Stour Trust/John Marriage Collection: 7 (bottom); Royal Holloway College, University of London: 17 (bottom); Science Museum, London: 14 (bottom), 15 (right), 16 (centre), 26 (bottom); the Shaftesbury Society – from *The Annual Outing and Other Excursions* by Alan Delgado (Allen & Unwin): 43 (top); Southwold Venture: 39 (left); *S. S. Great Britain* Project: 25 (bottom); St Katharine-By-The-Tower Ltd, a Taylor-Woodrow subsidiary company: 8 (top left); Suffolk County Record Office, Bury St Edmunds: 23 (bottom), 46 (right); Syndication International: 18 (top); Tramway Museum, Crich: 20 (bottom); Victoria and Albert Museum – Crown Copyright: 37 (top), 46 (centre).

Thanks are due to the Museum of London for the photographs on the following pages: cover, 3 (bottom left), 5 (top), 9 (centre), 12 (top left), 16 (top left), 18 (centre), 24 (top), 28 (centre), 29, 33 (bottom), 37 (bottom), 42 (top right and bottom), 45 (top and bottom). The pictures of Victorian horses and carriages on page 4 are from *Victorian Horses and Carriages: A Personal Sketchbook* by William Francis Freelove, published by Lutterworth Press, produced by Ventura Publishing Ltd. Copyright © illustrations by D. L. Jens Smith 1971, 1979. The pictures on pages 35 (left) and 43 (left) are from *East London* by Walter Besant (Chatto and Windus, 1903). The illustration on page 10 (top) was drawn by Jenny Mumford.

The extract on page 35 from *Clean Clothes on Sunday* by Celia Davies appears by permission of the publishers, Terence Dalton Ltd.

Every effort has been made to trace the ownership of copyrights; the Publishers will be glad to rectify any omissions in future impressions.

Thomas Nelson and Sons Ltd
Nelson House   Mayfield Road
Walton-on-Thames   Surrey KT12 5PL
P.O. Box 18123   Nairobi   Kenya

116-D JTC Factory Building
Lorong 3   Geylang Square   Singapore 1438

Thomas Nelson Australia Pty Ltd
19–39 Jeffcott Street   West Melbourne   Victoria 3003

Nelson Canada Ltd
81 Curlew Drive   Don Mills   Ontario M3A 2R1

Thomas Nelson (Hong Kong) Ltd
Watson Estate   Block A   13 Floor
Watson Road   Causeway Bay   Hong Kong

Thomas Nelson (Nigeria) Ltd
8 Ilupeju Bypass   PMB 21303   Ikeja   Lagos

© Richard Dunning, 1981
First published in 1981

ISBN 0 17 435023 6

NCN 3288 24 0

Phototypeset in Great Britain by
Filmtype Services Limited, Scarborough

Printed and bound in Hong Kong

Life and death

This memorial stone comes from a church at Bulmer in Essex. Notice that parents, daughter and grand-daughter all died in the same village.

Rowlandson's *The Overset*

For most people in the early nineteenth century it was still unusual to move away from the village they were born in. Try to find out where your parents and grandparents were born. Has your family always lived in the same town or village? Most families move around today much more than they used to 150 years ago.

This picture of a horse and carriage overturning gives you some idea of the difficulties of travel in the eighteenth century. Mud roads, that cracked in the summer and became impassable after heavy rain, were a great disadvantage. Perhaps you can now begin to understand why many people stayed in their birthplaces throughout their lives.

Traffic was increasing, and at the end of the eighteenth century roads began to improve as surfaces were made better. Look at the picture of an improved road in north London in 1819. This was called a turnpike or toll road. It should give you a clue as to how the money was raised to keep the roads in good repair.

By the beginning of the nineteenth century road travel had improved enough to allow regular, fast stagecoaches to use the turnpikes. Was there a turnpike road near where you live? Try to find out about the stagecoaches that used it and where the toll houses (the places where the money was collected) were situated.

◀ Islington Turnpike, 1819

The age of the horse

Nowadays we are very used to the motor car. What do you think the children in the picture are thinking and feeling? Children in Victorian times had a different sort of traffic to cope with.

The carriages in the pictures, below left, would be familiar if you lived in Victorian Britain. What has replaced them today? Draw a series of pictures showing these replacements.

The model stagecoach, above right, which can be seen at the Museum of London, is a copy of one that took the mails and some passengers from London to Holyhead. Would you rather have travelled inside or out?

One famous stagecoach operator was Mrs Nelson of the Bull Inn, Aldgate, in London. She seems to have been very strict with the men who drove her coaches. If a coachman drove his team into the Bull yard ten minutes late he was fined half a crown (12½p). Any greater delay could mean instant dismissal. She also found a way of dealing with rivals. When a competitor started up between London and Ipswich she cut her fares. By the end of the price cutting war she was carrying her passengers for nothing and giving them a free dinner at Witham. Her rival quickly went out of business!

Do you think Halifax was a pleasant place to live in, in the early nineteenth century? Apart from London, many towns in the north of England, South Wales and Central Scotland were growing very quickly at this time. Many factories were being built near the centres of these towns. Richer people wanted to 'escape'. They still had to work in the cities and towns, but they wanted to live elsewhere. Can you think how the road improvements helped them? Do a survey to find out how far the parents of your friends and classmates live from their place of work. Find the average distance. Why would it have been impossible for most people to live any distance from their workplace before 1800?

MILK CART

3 HORSE OMNIBUS

Model of London to
Holyhead stagecoach ▶

Halifax, early 19th
century
▼

Water remains a vital means of transport

What is powering the tourist barge in the picture above left?

Have a look at the picture showing the state of the roads in eighteenth-century Britain on page 3. Can you think why men who owned coal mines and factories were looking for better ways to move their heavy products? Barges on rivers had been used to move heavy goods, but often coal mines were not near rivers. In 1761 the Duke of Bridgewater, who owned a coal mine near Manchester, had a canal built linking his mine with the town. Until then he had had to use pack horses to transport his coal. After the canal was built, the Duke was able to sell his coal much more cheaply than his rivals and he made a lot of money. Not surprisingly, many other canals were built.

Modern barges are powered by diesel oil. What is powering the barges in the picture above right?

Try tying a piece of string to a small heavy object and pulling it along the ground. Place the object on a piece of wood and pull it through the water. Which is easier? Now you can see how much easier it was for a horse to pull a heavy load in a barge than in a cart.

▲ Opening of the Grand Union Canal, 1801

Canals and navigable rivers, 1850 ▶

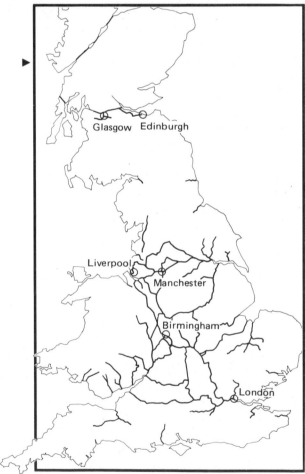

This map shows the canal and navigable (that is, able to carry barges) river network in about 1830. Most large towns were connected to each other and to the sea by water. This allowed heavy goods to be transported much more easily. See if you can find out more about any canals in your neighbourhood.

Locks and aqueducts were found on many
canals. The pictures above should tell you
what purpose they served.

In some places existing rivers were made into
'canals' in the eighteenth and early
nineteenth centuries. The picture on the right
shows the old quay building at Sudbury in
Suffolk. Once it was used for storing grain
before it went downstream. Now it is used as
a theatre. It was possible to reach Sudbury
from the sea, 35 miles away. Barges brought
goods, such as coal and iron, up the river and
took back wheat, oats, barley and
locally-made bricks.

The Quay, Sudbury,
Suffolk ▶

Pictured below are some of the barges that
used the River Stour. One of the bargemen
was named William Cardy. He was born at
The Quay, Sudbury and as a boy he led the
barge horse for his father, earning a penny a
day. The wage of the skipper was about one
pound for the two-day journey from Sudbury
to the sea. One Christmas, Cardy's father
lent him to another skipper. William was
pleased, because he was to be paid properly
for the first time. Halfway down the river the
floods were so high that it was unsafe to let
the water into the lock. The skipper left
William to look after the cargo and rode off.
Eventually the boy became hungry, and
finding a stack of grey peas nearby he boiled
them up and made a pease pudding. This
was his Christmas dinner!

Barges at Nayland,
Suffolk, 1905
▼

Barges were mainly used for transporting
goods. Can you think why they never
became popular for passenger travel?

The docks of the world

St Katharine's Dock, London, 1980 ▼

Opening St Katharine's Dock, London, 1828 ▲

On the last page we saw how important water was for moving heavy goods. During the early years of the nineteenth century, Britain's trade was increasing greatly. Other countries wanted Britain's cheap goods: Britain wanted more and more food and materials from overseas.

By 1800 the port of London was the busiest in the world. Ships waited down river for a space at the crowded quays and wharves. From 1802 onwards new large docks were constructed alongside the River Thames to the east of London. Look at the picture showing the opening of the St Katharine's Dock in 1828. Today some of these docks are derelict and empty and most of London's trade is handled at Tilbury, which is nearer the sea. Can you think why? Look at the modern picture. What has St Katharine's Dock become today?

Docks in the nineteenth century were exciting places. Exotic goods arrived from many parts of the world. At the London Docks a trade was established in bringing in foreign wines. Richer customers were invited to the docks to taste the 'wares'. A visitor in the 1860s described the scene: 'Different parties were going from cask to cask, from hogshead to hogshead, trying each vintage, and tasting brandies, and gins, and wines to the heart's content.' Not surprisingly, with all the temptation, the visitor's friend ended up being carried to a cab!

I.R. and G. Cruickshank's *Tom, Jerry and Logic "Tasting" Wine in the* *Wood at The London Docks*, 1821 ▼

Tobacco warehouse, London Docks, 1860 ▲

Below left is a scene from the docks in Victorian London: look at the men opening casks and cutting up tobacco. Many of the goods arrived in barrels and casks. One cooper described his job in the docks:

> . . . it was like geography come to life. At St Katharine's Docks we handled ivory from Africa and perfume from France; at Cutler Street, Persian carpets. . . at the Surrey Docks, German barrels of apple pulp; at the Victoria and Albert Docks we handled melons from Spain, peaches from Italy, tobacco in hogshead.

Do you think modern dockers see the goods they handle?

During the nineteenth century Britain ruled more and more of the world. By the end of the century the British Empire was at its greatest. Much of the trade was with parts of the Empire like Australia, Canada and India. Look at the map of the British Empire and try to list the countries which were a part of it in 1900.

Some of the goods imported in the nineteenth century are shown in the display on the right from the Museum of London.

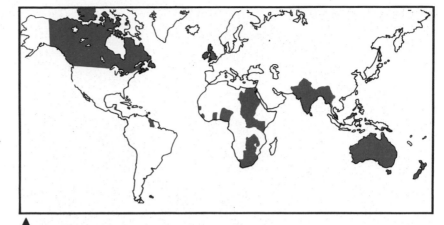

▲ British Empire, 1900

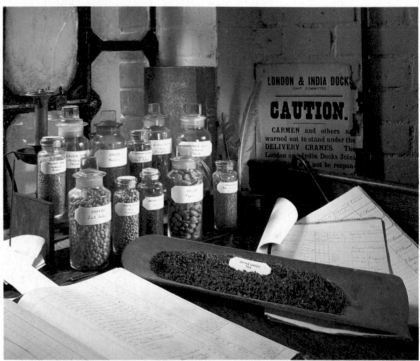

Look at the picture of the *S.S. Great Eastern*. Can you notice the two different ways by which it was powered? By the middle of the nineteenth century more and more steamships were taking over from sailing ships. What advantages would steamships have over the sail? Why do you think that many steamships, like the *S.S. Great Eastern*, continued to keep sails?

◀ *S.S. Great Eastern*, c. 1858

The railway revolution

The Liverpool and Manchester Railway, 1830 ▼

How are these children reacting to the arrival of this strange visitor? When the first steam locomotive arrived at Barrow in Furness in 1846 the local newspaper reported:

It was some time before the local children plucked up enough courage to approach the 'iron monster' and when the steam was first raised they fled in terror screeching and yelling.'

More than any other transport improvement it was the steam railway that changed Britain in the nineteenth century. The improvement of the steam locomotive allowed the merchants of Liverpool and Manchester to pay for a railway to be built. This railway, the first steam passenger line in the world, was opened in 1830.

Fanny Kemble was an early traveller on the railway in 1830:

We were introduced to the little engine which was to drag us along the rails. She consisted of a boiler, a stove, a small platform, a bench, and behind the bench a barrel to prevent her being thirsty for fifteen miles. She goes upon two wheels, which are her feet, and these are turned by bright, steel legs called pistons which are propelled by steam. The reins, bit and bridle of

◀ Richard Trevithick

George Stephenson ▶

this wonderful beast is a small handle which applies or withdraws the steam from its legs or pistons. The coals, which are its oats, were under the bench.

The Liverpool to Manchester Railway was a great success and the idea of building railways to link cities and towns quickly caught on. By 1851 there were seven thousand miles of railway in Britain. Can you think of any groups of people who would not be keen on railway building? Look back to pages 5 and 6 for clues.

Four of the greatest railway pioneers are pictured below. Try to find out how they developed the steam engine and engineered the first railways. Your local library should have some useful material.

Who owns all the main railways in Britain today? In Victorian times they were built and owned by many different companies. Some, like the Great Western, were very large; others, like the Isle of Wight Central, very small. Each railway had its own coat of arms which was depicted on the locomotives. Look at those pictured above. Try to find out where the four railway companies operated. Draw a coat of arms for an imaginary railway in your area.

On certain routes between the larger cities, two or more companies had different routes and competed with each other for business like supermarkets in the High Street today. How could one company attract passengers from another? Design a poster for one railway which is trying to attract passengers from a rival company.

Try to find out about the history of railways in your area. When were they built? Which companies owned them?

◀ Robert Stephenson

Isambard Kingdom ▶
Brunel

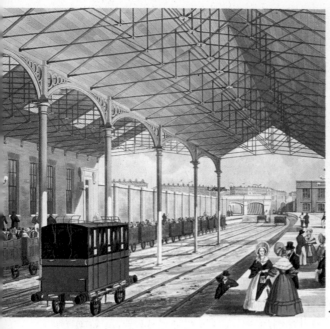

Rich and poor on the steam railway

The picture on the left shows one of British Rail's luxurious high speed trains. Can you find out on which routes they run? Compare this picture with that of Euston Station, London, in the 1830s. Look particularly at the coaches and wagons passengers had to travel in.

◄ Euston Station, London, 1830s

Queen Victoria's railway coach ▼

▲ Travelling to the Epsom Races, 1847 ▼

The early railway companies cared little for the comfort of their poorer passengers. Depending on how much you could pay you had to travel first, second or third class. Some railways even had four classes. Look at the differences in the ways first and third class passengers were carried to the Epsom Races in the 1840s.

Not even the first class passenger could expect this amount of luxury. This coach shown on the left was built for Queen Victoria by the London and North Western Railway. You can see it at the National Railway Museum, York. See how the ceiling and sides are quilted in white and blue silk and the floor is covered with thick carpet.

Look back to page 10 and remind yourself how the children of Barrow in Furness reacted to the sight of a steam locomotive. Many people in Britain were very frightened at the thought of rail travel. It was not until 1842 that Queen Victoria ventured on a train for the first time: she was very cautious and insisted on looking round the station and the coaches, asking questions about the safety of everything. The Queen travelled from Slough to Paddington, where she was met by a detachment of soldiers. Prince Albert was there to help her from her coach. Outside the crowds cheered; in the station the railwaymen sighed with relief. Can you think why the railwaymen were so relieved? Afterwards, the Queen wrote:

Buckingham Palace
14th July 1842

We arrived here yesterday morning, having come by the railroad from Windsor, in half an hour, free from dust and crowd and heat, and I am quite charmed with it.

What effect do you think the fact that the Queen had dared to travel on a train would have had on the rest of the population?

As the century progressed, rail travel became faster and much more comfortable for everyone. Express trains connected all the major towns and cities of Britain. In 1893 a Suffolk man, J. Ritchie, recollected the changes the railways had brought about in his lifetime:

I am old enough to remember how placid was the country, how stay-at-home were the people, what a sensation there was when anyone went to London, or any stranger appeared in our midst. From afar we heard of railways, then we had a railway opened from London to Brentwood; then the railways spread all over the land. . . the turnpikes were deserted; the inns were empty of customers; no longer did the villagers hasten to see the coach change horses, and the bugle of the guard was heard no more.

Now look at the picture of the enormous Great Western Royal Hotel. Travellers, and there were now many more of them, needed somewhere to stay and the railway companies built large hotels at their stations. Read through the advertisement. Is there a feature mentioned that we would take for granted?

The Great Western Hotel, ▶
London, 1900

▲
Steam locomotive on the Bluebell Railway, Sussex, 1890s

The construction of the railways

Do you live in an area that has been disrupted like the one in the picture on the right? In built up areas, the building of motorways often means that houses have to be demolished. Imagine that you were watching this scene and you used to live in one of the houses. What would your feelings be?

The scene below shows the building of the London and Birmingham Railway at Camden, just north of Euston, in 1836. Charles Dickens, in his book *Dombey and Son*, wrote:

> *Houses were knocked down; streets broken through and stopped; deep holes and trenches dug in the ground; enormous heaps of earth and clay thrown up; buildings that were undermined and shaking were propped by great beams of wood.*

What differences do you notice about the ways in which a modern road is constructed

and the way the railway at Camden was being built? One thing you should have noticed is the enormous number of men employed at Camden. The men who actually did the work were called navvies.

Railway construction, 1836
▼

14

Below left is a picture of some navvies photographed in south London in 1853. Sometimes three thousand or more would arrive in a district to lay the line of a railway. They built tunnels and cuttings to carry the railway through hills; embankments and viaducts to carry it over the valleys. Can you think why railways, unlike the improved roads, needed such large earthworks?

The death rate among the navvies was high. Many employers believed it was better to risk a navvy's life rather than take expensive precautions. Dynamite was often used on short fuses to save time. Digging tunnels was particularly dangerous work. Flooding and cave-ins were always a risk. Look at the picture of the navvies digging the Kilsby Tunnel between London and Birmingham. Try to find out how modern tunnels are constructed.

Many navvies were Irishmen who had come to England after the potato famine to look for work. There was often resentment felt against the Irish navvy gangs and sometimes these developed into large-scale riots. Here is a navvy song called *The Bold Navvy Man*:

> I've navvied here in Scotland, I've navvied in the south,
> Without a drink to cheer me or a crust to cross me mouth,
> I fed when I was workin' and starved when out on tramp.
> And the stone has been me pillow and the moon above me lamp.
> I have drunk me share and over when I was flush with tin,
> For the drouth without was nothin' to the drouth that burned within,
> And where'er I've filled me billy and whene'er I've drained me can,
> I've done it like a navvy, a bold navvy man.
> And I've done me graft and stuck it like a bold navvy man.

Apart from the violence and rough ways of the navvies there were other aspects of the railways that some people disliked. One of Charles Dickens' characters in *Dombey and Son* says:

> I left Dullborough in the days when there was no railroads in the land: I left in a stagecoach. I was shunted back the other day by train. . . and the first discovery I made was that the station had swallowed up the playing field. It was gone. . . the two beautiful hawthorn trees, the hedges, the turf and all those buttercups and daisies had given place to stony roads; while beyond the station an ugly dark monster of a tunnel kept its jaws open as if it had swallowed them and was greedy for more destruction.

See if you can paint or draw before-and-after pictures of these scenes.

▼ Railway navvies, 1853

Building the Kilsby Tunnel, 1837
▼

Model of Euston Arch

Euston Station, London, 1980

The picture on the left shows the circulating area of Euston Station in London today. Compare it with the picture of Euston in the 1830s on page 12. Euston is an unusual railway station. It was completely rebuilt in the 1960s. Look at the picture of Charing Cross Station, built in the 1860s. Most of our railway stations were built in Victorian times. During the rebuilding of Euston Station the fine arch in front of the old station was demolished. The model of the arch shown in the picture is in the Museum of London. Robert Stephenson was the engineer of the Euston to Birmingham Railway. The arch was a symbol of the success of the railway. Many railway stations, even those in country areas, were built on a grand scale.

Look at the picture of Caersws Station in mid-Wales. This is not grand, but it is well

Charing Cross Station, London, 1860s

Caersws Station, Wales, 1978

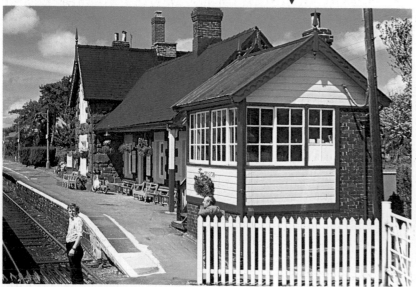

kept and adequate for the small community it serves. It was built in Victorian times for the Cambrian Railway. Since the early 1960s many railway stations have been closed completely or have lost all their staff and become halts. Can you think why this has happened?

Railway stations became a centre of town and village life in Victorian times. Farmers, shopkeepers and factory owners brought or collected goods and parcels; travellers bought their tickets. Make a list of other services which would have been provided at most railway stations.

Railway stations were exciting places in Victorian times. To many people standing on, for example, York Station, the announcement of a train to Aberdeen would seem as exotic as a flight to Hong Kong today. Have you ever spent a day at a railway station or airport? Write a story or poem about your impressions.

The famous picture below, painted by W.P. Frith in 1862, shows Paddington Station in London. See how many of these people you can find in it:

1 A fat railway enthusiast talking to the engine driver.
2 The harassed, lower-middle class family going on holiday for the first time.
3 An upper-middle class family seeing its boys off to boarding school.
4 The rich man arguing with the cabby about the fare.
5 A soldier kissing his plump baby goodbye.
6 A wedding party.
7 Police officers arresting a criminal.
8 A group of poor people returning home.

Imagine that you are one of the people in this busy scene. Write a story about Paddington Station and your journey. Perhaps you could draw or paint a similar group of people found on a station today.

Frith's *The Railway Station*, 1862
▼

Human moles

Prince Charles opened this new London Underground railway in 1979. Do you know what it is called? In 1829 a cartoonist drew a picture showing all kinds of weird gadgets and contraptions for transport. Can you draw a cartoon or make a list of inventions which would seem equally strange to us today? The cartoonist has not included an underground railway and yet, only forty years later, one was being built.

As London grew in size there were more and more traffic jams. In 1860 only one London station, Fenchurch Street, was in the City of London. One solution was to extend railways closer to the centre of London. In the picture below the Charing Cross extension is under construction. What do you think were the disadvantages of building a railway like this? Look back to page 14 to help you find the answer.

One disadvantage of this extension can be seen by reading this letter:

27th October 1862

Dear Sir,

The College Burial Ground and the Charing Cross Railway Company

I have now all the accounts of this matter and I send you a summary of them. I have been careful to keep down the cost, or it would have been double from the almost incredible number of bodies buried in the ground. . . There were at least 7,950 bodies removed. . . Finding the number so enormous and that the cost of separate removals would be so great, I did it wholesale and had 220 very large graves dug, each containing 26 human bodies. . . These were conveyed at night and the Cemetery Company made arrangements for them. . .

I remain, Dear Sir,
Yours faithfully,
Edward Hubershon, Architect

▲
Heath's *March of Intellect*, 1829

Building the Charing Cross extension in London, 1862 ▶

This letter is a grisly reminder of what further railway extensions into the hearts of cities would mean. Try drawing a picture or writing a play based on the opposition to the Charing Cross Railway Company and their proposed railway running through the burial ground.

The transport problems of London grew worse and worse. Many suggestions were made including: building overhead railways on arches right through the city; constructing a railway on a viaduct right down the middle of the River Thames; building a glass-covered avenue with railways and walkways right round London, to be called the Crystal Way.

A suggestion of burrowing right under London seemed to most people to be the stupidest idea of all. People joked about 'the underground railway' as though it was something quite fantastic. 'Let's all go underground' became the most popular funny song of the late 1850s. Some Londoners thought that the whole city would collapse, and one man even prophesied that an underground railway would enrage the heavens and bring the world to an end!

Look at the picture above of the first underground railway being built between Paddington and Farringdon. You should be able to work out what methods of construction were used. This way was called

Building the Metropolitan Railway in London, 1862

'cut and cover'. What problems do you think it caused both above and below the ground?

Look carefully at the picture below and see if you can guess why both driver and passengers were pleased that the railway came out 'in the air' so often. One journalist who used the Metropolitan Railway in the 1890s wrote:

The sensation was much like the inhaling of gas before having a tooth drawn. Visions of accidents, collisions and crumbling tunnels floated through my mind; a fierce wind took away my breath and blacks filled my eyes. I crouched low and held on like grim death.

◀ Early train on the Metropolitan Railway

The use of electricity

Did you know that trams are still in operation in Blackpool? Can you think why this town has kept its tram system? In late Victorian times many towns and cities developed their own tramways. As cities became bigger it was more and more difficult to travel from one part of the city to another. Horse-bus services were operating in London from 1829, and soon afterwards in other large towns.

A means of making city and town travel quicker and cheaper was first tried in Birkenhead in 1860. It was to lay rails along the streets and run horse-drawn trams on them. The picture shows one that you can still ride on today at the Crich Tramway Museum in Derbyshire.

The big advance in tram power came in Germany where, in 1881, electricity was used successfully to power trams. At first this proved to be very unsafe. The electricity actually ran through the lines in the street so anyone who walked across the line risked electrocution. Better versions were soon developed using plough-type devices to pick up the electricity from under the street. The most popular solution was to use overhead wires to carry the electricity. Leeds developed tramways like this from 1891 onwards and soon many other cities followed their example.

Blackpool trams ▶

Sheffield horse drawn tram, 1874
▼

Sheffield electric tram, 1899
▼

Sheffield had developed horse tramways from 1873 onwards. Look at the picture of the electric tram. It was built for the electrification of the Sheffield Tramways in 1899 and is still in operation at Crich. What advantages would electric trams have over horse or steam trams?

Electricity was not only used on the tramways. Look back to the picture of an early underground railway on page 19. Think why the use of electricity to power underground railways would be very helpful.

In the 1860s two men, Barlow and Greathead, developed a machine which allowed deep 'tube' railways to be built. Why would it have been difficult to operate steam trains on this type of railway?

In 1886 construction began on the City and South London Tube Railway. When the Railway was opened by the Prince of Wales in 1890 it was not steam, but electric engines, that powered the trains. Look at the picture of the inside of one of the coaches used on this line. This coach is now preserved at the London Transport Museum. Why did the company provide hardly any windows? These coaches quickly became known as 'padded cells'!

Though many people were frightened at the thought of travelling so far below ground level, the Prince of Wales' journey certainly helped the success of tube railways. Building the tube caused far less disruption than the 'cut and cover' railways had done. Soon other companies, like the Charing Cross, Euston and Hampstead, and the Central London Railway were proposing tube lines in all directions. By the end of Queen Victoria's reign the London tube system had begun to take shape.

The poster below was produced in 1908 after the end of Victoria's reign. You can see from the map, that the network had developed. Design a similar poster for today encouraging Londoners to travel by tube.

▲
The 'padded cell'

No Need to Ask a Policeman
▼

UNDERGROUND TO ANYWHERE

QUICKEST WAY CHEAPEST FARE

NO NEED TO ASK A P'LICEMAN!

Getting away from it all

Today over half of the families in Britain own a car. It is easy for most of us to escape from the cities and visit attractive places. What problems do you think so many cars and people cause?

In Victorian Britain only the very rich could afford their own private means of transport. Most rich families would own horses and carriages: some even owned railway coaches. Most people had to travel where the railways or tramways could carry them. Inventors had been experimenting with steam cars for many years but they were never a great success. It was not until the 1880s that two Germans, Daimler and Benz, perfected the ancestor of our modern motor cars. But in Britain, drivers of mechanical vehicles were forbidden to travel at more than four miles an hour. For a time a man with a red flag had to precede the vehicle.

Can you think why the government passed such strict regulations governing the use of motor vehicles? Motor enthusiasts were greatly opposed to these and protested against them. In 1896 the old law was changed and motorists were allowed to travel at twelve miles per hour. In celebration of this the Arnold Carriage, shown in the picture below left, and other cars took part in a drive from London to Brighton.

A Suffolk man, Gerald Dixon, aged 84 gave an interview in 1970 about his reminiscences of the early days of motoring in the 1890s and 1900s:

Q. *What were the roads like?*
A. *When I reached Norwich it was dust everywhere, and if you struck a wet day, there you were, covered with a wet soup.*
Q. *How did you get your petrol?*
A. *Petrol was in cans and you took a spare can with you. I always carried a spare.*
Q. *What did the local people think of the car?*
A. *Well they were interested, you see it was a novelty. The tops of the seats were black and the bodywork deep red.*
Q. *How did you get on with the law?*
A. *One day I was on my way to Cromer and there was a police trap at Wickham Market. When I got to the next village the old policeman stepped out and said I was doing 22 miles an hour. I had to go to Diss Court and was fined seven pounds.*

Look at the picture of the punctured tyre. This was a far more common problem for early motorists than it is today. Most roads were in a very bad state, especially those in the country. Can you think why this was so?

Arnold Carriage, 1896
▼

Mending a puncture, 1905
▼

Early motor cars were for the very rich. Another independent form of transport was cheap enough for large numbers of people to own. The bicycle was developed from the hobby horse which appeared as early as 1818. One Staffordshire farm labourer bought an early machine for half a crown (12½p) with a wooden frame and handlebars, but no chain or pedals! The idea was that you pushed it along the ground with your feet! Look at the series of cartoons entitled *The Joys and Problems of Riding the Penny Farthing*. It appeared in 1882. Early cyclists had many problems. Try to draw a series of cartoons to show the problems modern cyclists have.

By the 1890s bicycles were beginning to look like present-day models. Cycling clubs encouraged racing and allowed many young people to 'escape' into the countryside.

The Joys and Problems of Riding the Penny Farthing ▶

Bury Cycle and Athletic Club, Annual Race Meeting, 1898
▼

For you to see...

◀ Penny farthing, 1880
Museum of London

Steam Locomotive, 1897,
National Railway
Museum, York
▼

Knifeboard horsebus, ▶
1851, London Transport
Museum

S.S. Great Britain, 1843,
Bristol Docks
▼

Instant news

Today it is possible for us to go 'live' to the moon or even to the bottom of the sea. We are able to sit in front of a television set and discover what is happening in the rest of the world. Think of the most exciting live event you have ever watched on television.

Until the nineteenth century news travelled very slowly. Can you think how you could have found out what was happening in the rest of the world if you had lived in a small village? Important events, like the threatened invasion by Napoleon, would have to be signalled by a whole series of hilltop fires positioned throughout the country.

Early newspapers travelled in mail coaches and therefore 'London news' would take a long time to reach the rest of Britain. Newspaper reporters had to communicate the news to their head office in person. Charles Dickens wrote in 1831 when he was a nineteen-year-old newspaper reporter: 'I wrote on the palm of my hand, by the light of a dark lantern in a bumpy carriage, whilst galloping through a wild country at the dead of night.'

Some newspapers even employed pigeons for long distance news coverage! How does a newspaper reporter transmit stories to his editor today?

The spread of railways meant that London newspapers could reach the rest of the country much more quickly, but the railways could not help the newspaper reporter who often had to come all the way back to London with his story. Look at the picture of the inside of a railway signal box. You can see this at the Science Museum, London. Find out what the job of a railway signalman is. How do you think the equipment in a signal box could help the newspaper reporter with his news coverage?

◀ Interior of railway signal box

It was the perfection of the telegraph as a device for ensuring railway safety that also benefited the newspaper reporter. The telegraph system followed the railway lines and allowed short messages to be sent all over the country at a rapid speed. In 1844 *The Times* in London astounded its readers by publishing news of the birth of a baby to Queen Victoria at Windsor only four hours after it had happened.

The use of the telegraph quickly spread, and by the 1850s a channel cable connected Britain with the rest of Europe.

In 1866 a trans-Atlantic cable was laid, allowing direct communication between Britain and the Americas for the first time. The picture shows the cable ready for shipment.

Crime, as well as news reporting, was quickly affected by transport improvements and by the telegraph. In 1845 John Towell travelled down from Paddington to Slough to poison a woman who lived near the station. He thought that he would be back in London before the body was found. The woman drank the cyanide contained in stout but managed to scream before she died. Towell rushed off and caught the train. Back in London he travelled around a number of coffee houses to establish an alibi. Unfortunately for Towell a neighbour had heard the scream and the police, finding the woman's body, had quickly telegraphed Towell's description to Paddington. Towell did not realise that he had been trailed as soon as he arrived back in London. He was arrested the next day.

The trans-Atlantic telegraph cable
▼

A cheap, fast postal service

How do you think this girl is feeling? When it's your birthday you probably long for the postman to arrive. Do you keep your birthday cards? Try to make a list of all the different places your cards came from. Plot these places on a map. Which card came the furthest? Most of us take it for granted that the postman arrives every day with letters. Before Victorian times the postal system was very different.

The General Post Office, 1830

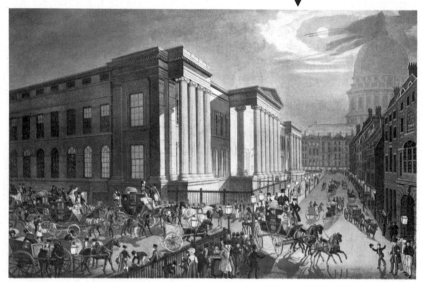

Post office coach interior, 1885

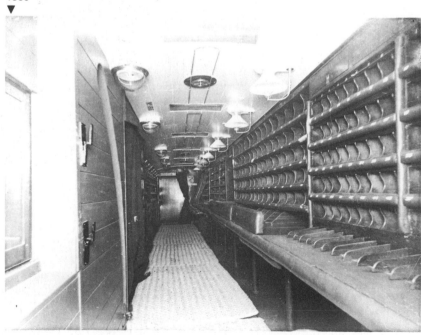

The picture below left shows the eight o'clock night mails leaving the newly-opened General Post Office in London in 1830. The mail coaches travelled through the night to all parts of the country. Look back to page 3 to see what sort of roads the coaches travelled on. The mail coaches were in too much of a hurry to stop and pay tolls. The coachman blew his horn and the gate was raised. This new type of Post Office quickly became outdated. Why do you think the age of the mail coach was shortlived?

In what ways would the railways be superior to stage coaches in moving letters about the country? The Post Office began using the railways as early as 1830. Look at the picture of a replica of a travelling post office of 1838. You can see this exhibit in the National Railway Museum in York. Can you see how mail could be collected without the train stopping?

As more railways opened they increasingly replaced the mail coaches. Letters were very cheap to send after Rowland Hill introduced the Penny Post. From 1840 the same postage was charged regardless of where the letter was going. By 1850 five times more letters were being sent. Find out about Rowland Hill and the Penny Post. If you write to the Postal Headquarters, St Martins le Grand, London EC1 1HQ they will send you some material.

The travelling post office shown in the picture below left was used on the west coast main line between London and Glasgow. It was built in 1885. All through the night postmen worked aboard the train sorting out letters. En route bundles of letters would be dropped off and collected without the train having to stop.

Post office coach, 1838

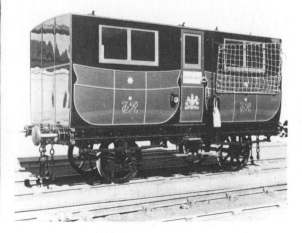

A cheap, fast, postal service encouraged people to write to each other. As people moved away from their birthplaces letters enabled them to keep in touch. Soon greetings cards also became fashionable. By 1875, 10,000 women were employed in trimming printed valentine cards with ribbon, paper, lace and flowers. The idea of greeting 'secret sweethearts' on February 14th became very popular. Look at the selection of cards pictured. They come from a collection of Victorian valentine cards in the Museum of London.

Victorian valentine cards
▼

A Valentine

You've heard of the fable
"The tortoise and hare"
The slow plodding tortoise
was "first to get there"
With marriage the goal,
You may yet be too late,
For M............
who might win,
M............
may not wait.

Dont let this 'ere hint
be lost upon you.!

J. KING, LONDON.

You think yourself fine, in your shiney cap,
But to have you I am not such a flat,
You astonish the town when you're ringing your bell
That the train is coming the passengers to tell,
And though you think you're the beau of the line,
I cannot have you for my Valentine.

London : Marks & Son
145

Food and markets

Try to make a list of all the different types of food and drink you consume in a three-day period. How much of it is produced near where you live? Compare your list with that of John Weir who lived in a Cumbrian village in 1810.

John Weir, his wife and three children lived at Dalston in Cumbria. John was a farmworker who earned £19 a year. His wife earned £2.25 by spinning flax and helping with the harvest. Their yearly budget (in decimal currency) was as follows:

Barley (some for pigs kept)	£5.00
Milk	£2.66½
Potatoes	£1.25
Butter	£1.33½
Oatmeal	£2.34
Tea, sugar, flour and other groceries	£2.00
Rent, coal, clothes, shoes and other expenses	£6.66
	£21.25

Which of the foods came from a distance? Did John and his family have much to spend on amusements?

Before the nineteenth century the householder depended mainly on local food supplies. During Victorian times a change took place. Today we depend on food from all over the world.

Small towns had had their own markets for hundreds of years. Farmers from surrounding villages would bring food they had to spare to sell at the market. There were already large markets at the beginning of Queen Victoria's reign in London and the other big towns. After the railways had opened the markets in London became centres of distribution for foods from the whole country. Find out for which commodities these London markets are known: Billingsgate, Smithfield, Leadenhall.

Covent Garden Market, London, 1830
▼

The central fruit and vegetable market in London was Covent Garden. Look at the picture on the facing page of the rebuilt market painted in 1830. Charles Dickens' son described the busy Covent Garden scene in the late nineteenth century:

All night long on the great main roads the rumble of heavy wagons seldom ceases and before daylight the market is crowded. . . If it be summertime, flowers as well as fruits are sold at the early markets. There are hundreds of women and girls purchasing bunches of roses, violets and other flowers. . . these are the London flower girls. . . In winter there are thousands of boxes of oranges, hundreds of sacks of nuts, boxes of Hamburg grapes and of French winter pears, barrels of bright American apples.

Already in Victorian times German grapes, French pears and American apples were arriving in large quantities.

Foreign fruit and grain reached Britain quickly and cheaply by fast steamship. Cheap meat reached Britain from as far away as Australia in refrigerated compartments. What effects do you think the arrival of all this cheap foreign food had on British farmers?

The picture below shows an upper-middle class Victorian family beginning breakfast. The servants, who got up at five-thirty to prepare the meal, joined the family for morning prayers.

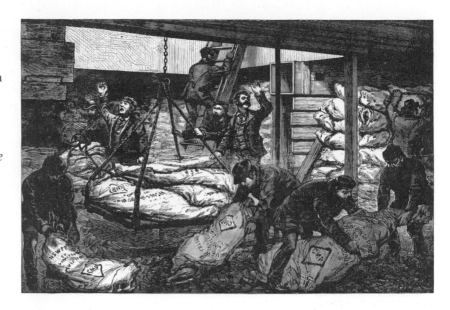

▲
Australian frozen meat arriving in London, 1881

A Victorian family breakfast
▼

Inside and out

'Let as fast as built'
▼

Have you seen any houses like these in your neighbourhood? These are three pictures representing architecture in Essex, Cheshire and Derbyshire. Can you match these styles up with the counties? Do you know your local style of architecture? Perhaps there no longer is one. Can you think how Victorian transport improvements affected the way in which houses were built and what they were made of? In pre-Victorian times it was most common for bricks and roof tiles to be made at small works and used nearby. Can you think why so much use was made of local products? In Victorian times more and more use was made of standard Fletton bricks and Welsh slates. Thus, the same type of house could be built cheaply up and down the country.

Today some districts are entirely made up of Victorian houses. New housing areas, like the one shown in the picture below right, were constructed around all the large towns and cities of Britain. Notice how many of the houses under construction were already let. Can you think why many people preferred to live in these houses? People still dream of living in a new house. Nowadays many Victorian houses are being knocked down, in their turn, and replaced with modern flats and houses. Do you think this is a good idea?

Can you find a Victorian area where you live? Try to mark the area on a local street map. Do you notice anything about the street pattern of this area? If you live in a village you will probably find few Victorian houses. Can you explain why?

Victorian parlour

Does the inside of the house on the left look familiar? Nowadays many people prefer to live in uncluttered surroundings which are easy to keep clean. In Victorian times the middle classes preferred to live in houses that were full of ornaments and decorations. The picture on the right shows the reconstructed Victorian parlour at the Castle Museum, York. Even the richer working classes could afford some of the articles that were cheaper imitations of the richer ornaments.

In Victorian times pictures, furniture and ornaments became much cheaper. Instead of being hand-made, goods were mass produced in factories. These goods could be moved about more economically because of cheap railway transport.

Look at the articles in the picture below. They were all made as souvenirs for the Great Exhibition which you will read more about on page 42. Can you identify them? Victorians loved to fill their homes with bric-à-brac. Would you like to look after the parlour in the picture? How long each day would it take to keep it spotlessly clean? Luckily for the Victorian middle and upper classes, servants were cheap and easy to find. Do you think the amount we pay cleaners has affected the way we plan our living rooms today?

Souvenirs of the Great Exhibition
▼

Work and rest

The period after 1750 brought about a great change in the working habits of most British people. Before 1750 the vast majority of people worked on the land, or at home in craft industries. From the middle of the eighteenth century more and more people began to work in factories and, in some areas, coal mines.

Conditions were extremely harsh for the early factory workers and miners. Even young children sometimes worked a sixteen-hour day. At the beginning of Queen Victoria's reign conditions were improving, but even in 1900 people were expected to work far longer hours and under harsher conditions than today. Look at some of the rules and regulations that had to be obeyed in a Lancashire cotton mill in 1851:

RULES TO BE OBSERVED BY THE HANDS EMPLOYED IN THIS MILL

Rule 2   Any person coming too late shall be fined as follows: for 5 minutes 2d, 10 minutes 4d, and 15 minutes 6d.

Rule 5   For waste on the floor 2d.

Rule 6   For any oil wasted or spilled on the floor 2d each offence, besides paying for the value of the oil.

Rule 9   Any person found leaving their work and found talking with any other of the workpeople shall be fined 2d for each offence.

Rule 10   For every oath or insolent language, 3d for the first offence, and, if repeated, they shall be dismissed.

Rule 12   All persons in our employ shall serve four weeks notice before leaving their employ; but L. Whitaker and Sons shall and will turn any person off without notice being given.

Rule 16   The Masters would recommend that all their workpeople wash themselves every morning, but they shall wash themselves at least twice every week, Monday morning and Thursday morning: and any found not washed will be fined 3d for each offence.

Rule 21   Any person wilfully damaging this notice will be dismissed.

Would your parents work in a factory under these conditions? Ask them if they have to obey any similar rules and regulations. Perhaps you could write a list of rules for you and your classmates to obey at school.

Workers leaving the factory 1980
▼

Workers leaving the factory, late nineteenth century
▼

Look at the picture of the station staff at Hethersett in Norfolk. For many, work on the railway was preferable to a long, hard, boring day in a factory. Can you think why? Railwaymen were usually proud of their work, but they had to work hard too. Most railwaymen worked at least a twelve-hour day. Railway porters were expected to arrive at six in the morning and remain until the last passenger had gone. Engine drivers and firemen had to work a return journey. If this was from London to Plymouth and back they would be working well over twelve hours a day. Many railway accidents in the 1860s were blamed on these long hours.

Railway workers at Hethersett Station, Norfolk, 1865 ▶

For most people the only complete day off was Sunday, 'the day of rest'. Sunday was far more religiously observed in Victorian times than it is today. Amusements and entertainments were frowned upon. There were many protests when the railways began to operate on Sundays. Many people thought that the only place to travel to was church. What differences are there now between Sundays and other weekdays? Make a list of them.

Read this description of a typical morning for a middle class Victorian child:

> On Sunday mornings, after father had wound up all the clocks, which we loved to watch, he would ask Nannie if he could take the children for a walk. No time must be wasted for he had to be home again in time to accompany mother to church at 11 o'clock. Nannie would bustle about and dress Barbara and me in our best bonnets and coats. Sunday clothes were quite different from week-day ones and all our underclothes were clean and stiff with starch!

To us, the way many Victorians spent their one day off would seem very boring. At least it was a time when people, like the husband and wife in the picture, could rest from all their hard work.

◀ Raven Hill's *A Quiet Dullness*, 1900

Heaven and hell

Today many people work a distance from where they live. Each day they have to travel by train, car or bus into large cities. What problems does this cause?

Look back to pages 3, 4 and 5 to remind yourself of the transport improvements that had made it possible for richer people to move further outside the larger cities but continue to work in them. The building of the railways allowed this process to go much further.

Below is a picture of the area around Kenley, Surrey, twelve miles from central London. The railway to London had been opened in 1856 and this picture was taken in about 1900. Perhaps you can guess what sort of people lived in these large, tree-surrounded houses. Richer people were able to move from the centres of the large cities. Look back to the picture of Halifax on page 5 to remind yourself of why they should leave. By the middle of the nineteenth century the railway allowed people to move twelve miles and more from their place of work. Villages and small towns on the railway routes out of cities like Manchester, London and Birmingham became suburbs of the large cities. A suburb is a place from which the majority of workers travel to a nearby city to work every weekday.

Life in the richer suburbs was lived to very strict, if unwritten, rules. Cut off from the cities where they worked, the men spent their weekends enjoying garden parties, bridge and whist parties, croquet, tennis, golf, cricket, football and rugby. The suburban ladies and their daughters had little to do after their husbands and fathers left on the morning train and they spent their time calling on each other and leaving visiting cards.

Kenley, Surrey, c. 1900
▼

Station from the Downs.

What were the effects of many of the rich leaving the large cities? The houses where the merchants and factory owners lived quickly became cheap offices, shops or even slums. Lambeth, in South London, is only eight miles from Kenley and yet the way of life was completely different. Railway travel and the growth of the fashionable suburb led to the rise of the one-class area. No longer did the factory owner live next door to his employees. What effects do you think this would have on the understanding between an employer and his workers?

Look at the picture of a lodging house in Holborn, London. People were living directly above an unlined cesspit. The diseases caused by such appalling conditions led to a very high death rate. Do you think these conditions might have been better if the richer people had not moved away?

In one part of Covent Garden in London in the late 1830s, 2,522 people were found to be living in a single acre. A doctor wrote, in 1851:

> *It is no uncommon thing, in 12 feet square or less, to find three or four families styed together, filling the same space night and day — men, women and children living like cattle.*

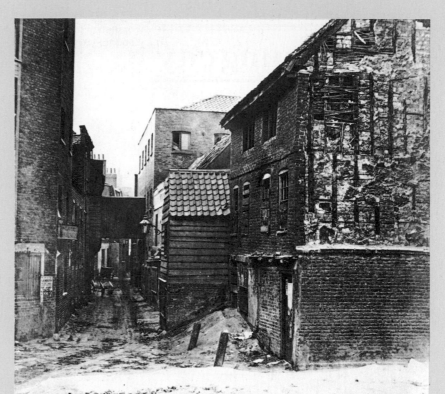

▲ Slum in Lambeth, London, 1860s

Find out how many people are accommodated per acre on a modern housing estate. Mark out a twelve-foot square area and see how many people you can cram into it.

Field Lane, Holborn, 1840s
▼

The booming city

The graph on the right should give you a good idea of how much London grew in the nineteenth century. Now look at the graph below showing population growth in other major towns.

By the end of Queen Victoria's reign more than half of the British people lived in towns and cities. The British had become townspeople and there were far more of them.

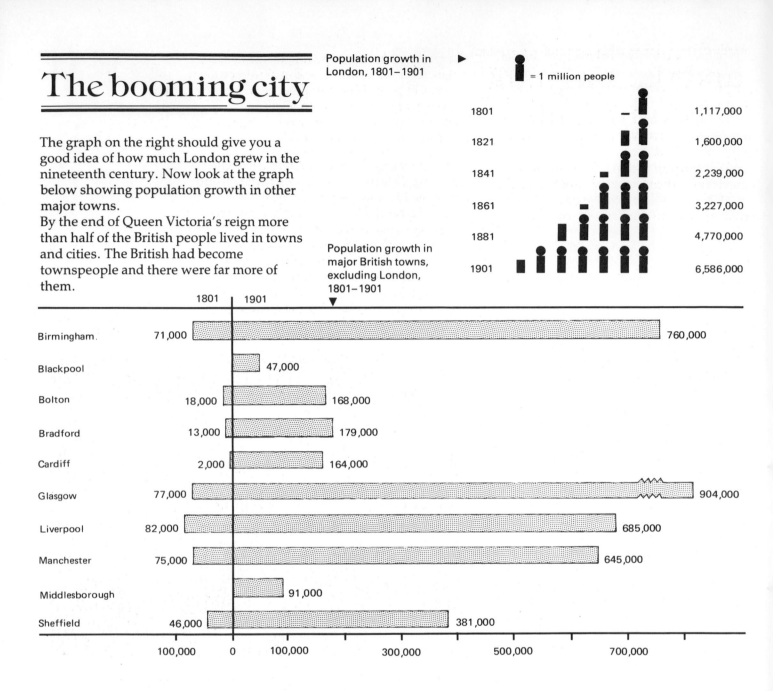

Population growth in London, 1801–1901 ▶

🌡 = 1 million people

1801	1,117,000
1821	1,600,000
1841	2,239,000
1861	3,227,000
1881	4,770,000
1901	6,586,000

Population growth in major British towns, excluding London, 1801–1901 ▼

Town	1801	1901
Birmingham	71,000	760,000
Blackpool		47,000
Bolton	18,000	168,000
Bradford	13,000	179,000
Cardiff	2,000	164,000
Glasgow	77,000	904,000
Liverpool	82,000	685,000
Manchester	75,000	645,000
Middlesborough		91,000
Sheffield	46,000	381,000

100,000   0   100,000   300,000   500,000   700,000

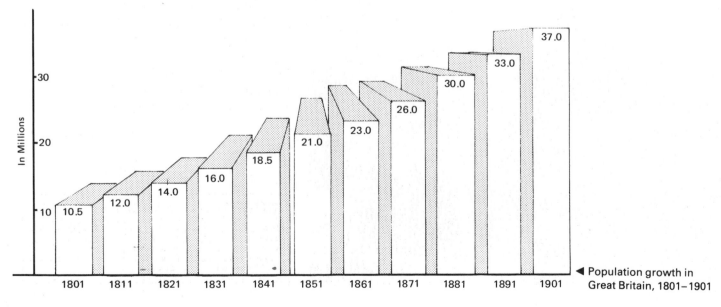

In Millions

1801	1811	1821	1831	1841	1851	1861	1871	1881	1891	1901
10.5	12.0	14.0	16.0	18.5	21.0	23.0	26.0	30.0	33.0	37.0

◀ Population growth in Great Britain, 1801–1901

and the stagnant countryside

Look at the population figures showing the great rise in the number of people from 1801 to 1901. Now look at the figures for three country parishes in Suffolk:

	1801	1901
Little Cornard	280	290
Newton	350	330
Edwardstone	360	420

What differences do you notice between the huge rise in population of the whole country and the change in country areas? Can you explain the differences?

While the population of the whole country increased almost four times in the nineteenth century, in many rural areas the population remained the same or even fell. Try to find out the population figures for your area in the last century. Your local record office should be able to help you.

Often country railways were much less fast and efficient than the main lines. Look at the cartoon of a Suffolk railway. How does the cartoonist show how few trains run? Many East Anglian branch lines had a reputation for being slow. One boy of sixteen discovered to be travelling at half fare pleaded that he had been twelve when the journey started!

In the countryside in the nineteenth century there were no factories, and communications were still poor. People depended on farming and the land, on the weather and the seasons. Machines had not yet changed people's way of life very much.

Transport improvements did much to end farming prosperity. Look back to the picture on page 31 showing foreign meat being unloaded at the London Docks. From about 1870 onwards foreign meat, wheat and butter began to arrive in Britain in huge quantities and at cheap prices. The farming depression, caused by cheap foreign food, led to many people leaving the country areas for the cities. Others preferred to leave Britain altogether and emigrate.

Life below decks on an emigrant ship, 1887
▼

Look at the picture of an emigrant ship in 1887. The journey was often very unpleasant but many thousands left Britain to make a better life overseas.

The British government encouraged emigration to Australia, Canada, New Zealand and South Africa.

Advertising for emigrants to Canada, London *Evening News*, 2 March 1900
▼

WANTED, EMIGRANTS FOR CANADA.—Farmers, Labourers, Servant Girls, &c.—For free pamphlets apply Passenger Department, Canadian Pacific Ry., 67 and 68, King William-street, E.C., or 30, Cockspur-street, S.W. Agency of Allan, American, Cunard, Dominion, Norddeutscher, White Star, &c.

Time and speed

Pictured on the right is David Springbett, a Briton who flew completely round the world in 1980, using scheduled airlines, in only 44 hours 6 minutes. In 1957 three American airmen flew round the world in 45 hours 19 minutes averaging 525 miles per hour. How do you think people living in Britain before Queen Victoria's reign would have felt about such speeds? Look back to the crazy future, on page 18, suggested by a cartoonist in 1829. Perhaps the cartoonist was nearer the truth than he thought possible!

Sir Robert Peel was in Rome in 1834 when he was asked to be Prime Minister. He set out to return as soon as he could. Even with specially hired light carriages, with the horses changed every few miles, it took him thirteen days to reach London. Find out how long an aircraft today takes to travel the same journey. Journey time was decreasing before Victorian times. In 1754 it took two days to travel from London to Birmingham by stagecoach; by 1785, only nineteen hours; by 1836, only eleven hours. How had these improvements been possible? Look back to page 3 if you cannot remember.

Copy out the table below and find out from a modern rail timetable today's fastest train for each route. Try to draw a line graph to illustrate your findings. On the vertical axis show the number of hours taken; on the horizontal axis show the dates. Use a different colour for each route and draw a key. From your graph, perhaps you can see more clearly why it could be said that Britain became much 'smaller' during Queen Victoria's reign.

Tom Tower Clock, Christ Church, Oxford ▼

TABLE OF JOURNEYS

Route	1836-Stagecoach	Time in hours 1850-Rail	1900-Rail	Today-Rail
London to Birmingham	11	3	2½	
London to Bury St Edmunds	9	4½	3	
London to Exeter	18	4¾	4	
London to Halifax	23½	7¼	4½	
London to Liverpool	24	6½	4¼	
London to Brighton	6	1¼	1¼	
London to Penzance	38	*27	8¾	
London to Edinburgh	43	12¼	8½	

*By rail, ferry and stagecoach

Look at the clock on the facing page. What is the time? No, you're wrong! This clock in Oxford still shows 'local' time. What do we mean by this? Today throughout the country we use Greenwich Mean Time or British Summer Time. Midday in the winter is when the sun is overhead at Greenwich, to the east of London. In 1841 the Great Western Railway Timetable noted: 'London time is 4 minutes earlier than Reading time, 7½ minutes before Cirencester and 14 minutes before Bridgewater.' It was 12 o'clock in each town when the sun was immediately overhead. The coming of the railways meant the end of local time. Greenwich or 'Railway' Time became accepted all over the country. Can you think why the railways did not like local time? How do you check that your watch is correct? How do you think the Victorians did this?

Why did farmworkers and villagers in the early nineteenth century have little use for the correct time? How would they have known when to start work? Country people depended on daylight for their work. Factory owners were not satisfied with this system. Look back to the factory regulations on page 34. Why do you think factory owners would want their employees to start work at certain times? It became more important to know what the time was, and clocks and watches became very common. Try to collect pictures of Victorian clocks and watches. Look at the three pictured here.

◀ Station clock, c. 1850

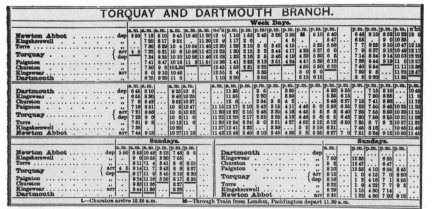

▲ Station clock showing 'railway time', c. 1850

Stationmaster's watch, 1865 ▼

Railways had to run their trains to a timetable. Otherwise people would not know when to arrive at the station. This is a copy of part of the Great Western Timetable of 1902.

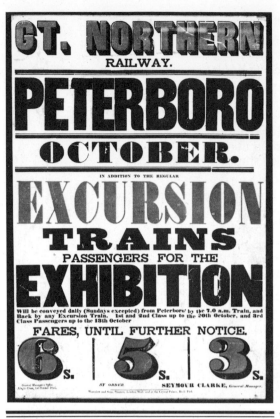

▶ Great Exhibition Railway
excursion poster

▲ Interior of the Great
Exhibition, Crystal Palace

The day out

Railway companies realised they could make money by encouraging large numbers of people to travel on special trains. In 1840 the Bodmin and Wadebridge Railway in Cornwall ran three extra trains so that the people of Wadebridge could watch William Lightfoot being hanged for murdering a certain Mr Norway. Half the population of Wadebridge, 1,100 people, travelled to Bodmin for the day!

The Great Exhibition,
Crystal Palace
▼

The Great Exhibition was housed in a specially-constructed building, made of iron and glass, known as the Crystal Palace. You can see a model of the building in the Museum of London. Look at the view of one small part of the inside of the exhibition hall. What exhibits can you see? The Great Exhibition demonstrated the triumph of steam power.

The Great Exhibition, held in Hyde Park in London in 1851, was a huge success. It was a celebration of Britain's achievement, full of machinery and products. Look at the Great Northern Railway poster advertising cheap trains to London. About four million people travelled to the Great Exhibition. Many of them brought back souvenirs like those pictured on page 33. Would it have been possible for so many people to visit London before the coming of the railways? One Huddersfield workman seemed to have had a real bargain: he left home on the night of July 22nd, paying five shillings (25p) for the third-class return fare. In his pocket were sandwiches, and a shilling (5p), which was the entrance fee. He ate his sandwiches at the exhibition, drank water from a fountain and returned home within forty hours of leaving.

Excursion trains became very popular in the nineteenth century. One early excursionist wrote to the first travel agent, Thomas Cook:

> *Dear Mr Cook,*
> *I wish it was in my power to tell you how much we owe you for these cheap excursions. Only think, for a few shillings I, as a poor working man, have been enabled to see the glories of the fine old city of York that I could never have seen but for your special train from Nottingham today.*

The railways made it possible for people who lived in the huge, smoke-filled cities to 'escape', if only for a few hours. Look at the picture of the British workman in Epping Forest, only eight miles from the grime of east London. Trees and grass were a real novelty for him.

In the 1880s and 1890s many charities and church groups were set up to take poor children out of the slums for the day. When the children arrived in the country they were fed and said prayers. This was followed by organised games. Children looked forward all the year to these special days. Can you remember a really good day out that you have had in the past?

◀ Raven Hill's *The British Workman in Epping Forest*

▲ A day in the country for London children, 1872

Prisoners in Mean Streets.

Tick off one square in a picture for every penny subscription. When you have all nine ticked, you have released one child from the prison bars of the slums for a day in the country.

SUBSCRIPTION FORM FOR PENNIES.

At the seaside

On hot, summer days you can see many crowded beaches like the one in the picture. Every year millions of British people visit the seaside. Can you think why few people visited the coast before the railway age? When the famous author, Charlotte Brontë, saw the sea for the first time at Bridlington in Yorkshire in 1839, she was 'quite overpowered, she could not speak until she had shed some tears and for the remainder of the day she was very quiet and exhausted'.

Before the nineteenth century the only people who visited or lived at the seaside were sailors and fishermen. Rich people in the eighteenth century often spent their leisure time in spa towns, like Bath and Harrogate, which had special waters that were supposed to cure all sorts of illnesses. It was the discovery of these waters at Scarborough on the coast that first attracted rich people to the seaside. See if you can find out more about spa towns and their waters. If you read Jane Austen's *Northanger Abbey* you will be able to learn what life was like in them.

By the early nineteenth century the idea of drinking and even bathing in sea water was becoming very fashionable. Look at the picture of Southend in 1822. There were already hotels for the visiting rich. Try to find the horse and covered wagon coming out of the sea. Can you think what it was for? What other attractions were being provided?

Daniell's *Southend Beach*, 1822
▼

Frith's *Ramsgate Sands*, 1851
▼

Apart from Scarborough and Southend, Brighton, Weymouth and Margate were also popular resorts for the rich classes. Would the building of railways affect these early resorts? Look at these figures for the numbers of people travelling from London to Brighton:

January-December, 1835 (stagecoach)

117,000

June-December, 1844 (train)   360,000

A day by the sea became popular with all classes in the nation.

Compare the picture of Ramsgate in Kent, in the 1860s with that of Southend in Essex, in the 1820s. Look again at the modern beach scene. What differences are there between the pictures?

Why were the railways very keen to encourage people to visit the seaside? At first, for most people, the trip to the seaside was for one day only. The habit of staying overnight increased, until by the end of the century a week by the sea was becoming possible for the richer working classes. Boarding houses were built to house the growing number of visitors. Other attractions like promenades, theatres and piers were built to encourage holidaymakers.

Have you a favourite seaside town? What special attractions has it for you?

It soon became popular to send postcards to friends and relatives at home showing and telling them what they were missing. Look at the collection of postcards which can be seen at the Museum of London. Try to make a similar collection of modern seaside postcards. Arrange them around a large map of Britain near the resort they show. Imagine you are a member of a Victorian family and have gone on your first seaside holiday. Write a postcard to a friend describing your experiences.

Travel for education, discovery and conquest

Holiday brochures today tempt us to take holidays abroad. What means of transport has enabled millions of Britons to take foreign holidays in the last thirty years? What attracts many British people to Spain rather than an English resort, like Blackpool?

Extract from Stanford's *Two Shilling Tourists' Guide*, 1887 ▶

...underfield Castle (marked on the maps) is supposed to have been the site of a house belonging, according to tradition, to King Athelstan.

Crowhurst Church is a small, but substantial structure. The door at the south porch, with its five oaken planks, iron bars across, iron cross at the top, and large iron scrolls proceeding from the hinges, is worth examination. Remains of painted glass in the east and also the north window. There are tombs and monumental brasses of the fifteenth century. On the floor of the chancel is an object

Ball-room at Hever.

Hever Castle

of some curiosity : on a cast-iron plate are embossed the figures of two boys, in one small square; over

Through *Oaktree clay*

Godstone.

Tandridge.

...tone. Stangrave, destroyed 1740. Bramc..., House, and Great Tingley are adjacent.

26¼ The village of **Godstone** is distant 2¼ miles from the Godstone station; the road to it winds round the base of Tilburstow Hill (a high sandy tract partly unenclosed, over which the hill road between Godstone and East Grinstead passes); the country north of the village is undulating, with ornamental timber. The grounds of Flower Hall and Rooksnest, with the hanging woods of Marden Park behind, form a scene of much softness and beauty, delectable for idling amongst. The delicious lane below the church is worn in the sandstone, and overhung with ivy and creeping plants. The church was thoroughly repaired and "ornamented" in 1839. Its tower is towards the east, on the south side. On the north side of the church, westward from the chancel, is a superb black and white marble altar-tomb, on which are finely executed figures of Sir John Evelyn and his lady, at full length; he in armour, she in a loose gown.

Tandridge had a priory of Austin canons, long since destroyed. Tandridge Hall (which formed part of the grant of Henry VIII. to John Ride, in exchange for Oatlands, near Weybridge,) has been repaired, but many of the rooms are ancient, and appear to be nearly in their pristine state. Tandridge Church stands on a green knoll, surrounded by clumps of trees; the enormous yew tree at the west end making it appear very small. The chancel is separated from the nave by a romanesque arch; on the right of the entrance, by the south porch,...

	¼ descend 1 in 264	
SURREY		SURREY
Crowhurst to	¼ level	Stafford's Wood
KENT	30	KENT
	¼ descend 1 in 264	
	31	
Hever 3½ miles CHIDDINGSTONE 5	Edenbridge	descend 1 in 2,640 WESTERHAM 5 miles BRASTED 7
		descend 1 in 406
	32	
	¼ Westerham Church on hill	
	¼ level	
	33	
	¼ descend 1 in 264	

▲ Railway travelling chart, 1846

The Victorians found travelling very exciting. Look at the picture map on the left. It describes in great detail what you would see from both sides of a railway carriage if you travelled on a train from London to Tunbridge Wells. This chart shows only a 4½ mile section of the journey. The total journey was 45 miles. There would be no chance to get bored if you were following your route on a map like this! How do you pass your time on long journeys?

Look at the advertisements for guide books which appeared in 1887. Many Victorian travellers were interested in history, geology, geography and biology. When you next go on holiday try to collect information on the area you visit and make up a scrapbook when you return home. Visit a Tourist Information Office. They often provide free brochures.

It was rare for ordinary people to travel abroad but rich Victorians did begin to desert the British beaches for the quiet of the French coast. Can you think why this happened? Look back to the two pictures of Southend and Ramsgate on page 44 to find a clue.

By late Victorian times some daring Britons were venturing even further abroad. Look back to page 39 to remind yourself of one group. Others visited India, China, South America for pleasure.

Design a poster to encourage rich Victorians to visit China or India.

ORIENT Co's PLEASURE CRUISE BY THE S.S. "LUSITANIA" TO THE WEST INDIA ISLANDS, MADEIRA, TENERIFFE, AZORES &c. FROM LONDON 16th January, 1895 for a 60 DAYS CRUISE

Improved travel by steamship and rail also allowed Britain to bring under her control large areas of the world. Look back to the map of the British Empire in 1900 on page 9. Explorers and discoverers set out from the safety of Britain to explore the interior of Africa, then almost unknown to Europeans. Among these travellers were David Livingstone and Cecil Rhodes. Both men did much to extend British Rule over Africa. Look at the cover of the book, *The Life and Explorations of Dr Livingstone*. David Livingstone was a missionary as well as an explorer, and it was his dream to spread Christianity throughout Africa. Try to discover more about the life of Livingstone. Your local library should be able to help you.

The rule of Britain over India and large parts of Africa led to British engineers travelling abroad to plan railways.

Cover from the book, *The Life and Explorations of Dr Livingstone* ▶

Construction of a railway in Egypt in the 1890s
▼

The age of steam and speed

These pictures, published in 1897, show clearly the changes in transport that occurred during the nineteenth century. The Victorian age of steam and speed replaced a slower age of horse and sail and moved us much closer to the mobile life style of today.